EVEN HERE

ALSO BY MICHAEL CERVAS

Inside the Box (poems, 2007)
Captivated (poems, 2011)
A Wilderness of Chances (poems, 2015)

EVEN HERE

Poems by

Michael Cervas

Antrim House
Bloomfield, Connecticut

Copyright © 2020 by Michael Cervas

Except for short selections reprinted for purposes of
book review, all reproduction rights are reserved.
Requests for permission to replicate should
be addressed to the publisher.

Library of Congress Control Number: 2019956564

ISBN: 978-1-943826-65-0

First Edition, 2020

Printed & bound by Ingram Conent Group

Book design by Rennie McQuilkin

Front cover watercolor by Kerry Kendall:
"At the Edge, Findhorn Bay, Scotland"

Author photograph by Scott Stevens

Antrim House
860.217.0023
AntrimHouseBooks@gmail.com
www.AntrimHouseBooks.com
400 Seabury Dr., #5196, Bloomfield, CT 06002

*For Brendan, Ryan, and Eloise:
May you always know that even here,
wherever you are, there is light and love.*

Acknowledgments

First of all, deepfelt thanks to Brian Ford, whose wise readings and judicious comments helped shape many of the poems in this book and who, when the author despaired of finding a way to choose the poems for this book, read through nearly two hundred poems to help him cull the ones he finally selected.

Gratitude also to everyone in the Westminster Artists Collective (musicians, dancers, artists, architects, and writers) for wonderful feedback on a number of these poems and for together cultivating a community committed to creative expression of all kinds.

Special thanks also to Westminster School, the Gordon McKinley Fund, and the Ford-Goldfarb English Department Enrichment Fund without whose support this book would not have been possible.

For friends and family who have supported me in so many ways, blessing and gratitude, now and forever.

Finally, for Deb without whose unconditional love these poems would simply not be because I would not be. You are my light. You are my life.

Table of Contents

I. SETTING OUT

Setting Out / 5
September in the Rain / 6
Squinting / 7
First Basket / 8
Grandma's Words / 9
Learning to Dance / 10
Proof Positive / 11
The Age of Transistors / 13
Escape / 15
That's Christmas to Me / 16
Christmas Lights / 18
My Friend's Granddaughter Discovers Rain / 19
Changing Names / 20
Song for January 2 / 21

II. LESSONS OF THE GAME

The Infidels Come to Church / 25
Lessons of the Game / 27
Watching My Son Bathe His Son / 32
Altars / 33
Consciousness Bars / 34
Living in a Poem / 36
Bagging a Deer / 37
Only a Rat's Life / 39
Birds of New Zealand / 40
Foolish Assumptions Again / 41
Sunflowers / 42
My Grandson Sends Me a Text Message / 44
Pickup Game on Elmgrove Street / 45

III. LAST LIGHT

Last Light / 49
Seeing My Father Again / 50
An Ordinary Evening in Hartford / 51
On Books and Death / 53
First Snow / 54
Bent Rims and Flat Tires / 55
Sooner or Later / 56
Going Under / 57
Skin on Skin / 59
The Cells of Your Heart / 60
The Milky Way / 61
The Garden in September / 64
Night Light / 65
Sleep Machine / 66
Surprise / 67

About the Author / 69
About the Book / 70

*Not knowing when the Dawn will come,
I open every Door
Or has it feathers, like a Bird,
Or Billows, like a Shore—*

                                    Emily Dickinson

*Open your eyes and see what you can with
them before they close forever.*

                                    Anthony Doerr

Even Here

I. SETTING OUT

Setting Out

The first push into surf
        against the thrashing winds
                with only obscure prophecies

of undiscovered lands
        to stand against such
                endless oceans of fear,

the first note of a song
        A sharp or B flat, the keys
                to altogether different tunes,

their vibrations pulling
        new worlds into existence
                as sounds swirl and swirl,

the very first time
        I reached under the table
                to touch your fingers there,

half terror, half thrill,
        a shattering of certainty
                at the instant of setting out.

September in the Rain

I am sitting here listening
to Roy Hargrove's "September
in the Rain" on Spotify,
a lovely and surprisingly upbeat
tune written in 1937 and introduced
in the movie *Melody for Two*—
and I am also staring out the window
at a rainy day, droplets speckling
the glass, the trees with leaves already
melting auburn and orange, waving
against the grey backdrop of clouds—
a film about a man who is walking
in springtime remembering raindrops
playing the sweetest of refrains
as he was falling in love in the fall.
My mother and father were married
on just such a drizzly September
day over seven decades ago, but
I'm not thinking about their marriage
now, a mostly happy old-fashioned
marriage with all the ups and downs
you'd expect in a love affair that lasted
for over forty years. No, instead
I am thinking about those two
fifteen-year-olds kids seeing that movie
for the first time, having first crushes,
first kisses, walking beside someone
in the September rain, their whole lives
still ahead of them, long before
either of them would come to see
the way life bends us all down at last
like trees in the rain in September.

Squinting

Whenever I need to read
the fine print
on the back of a capsule

of pills, or
whenever I want to check
the box scores

in the newspaper,
I take off
my glasses and put

my nose right
in front of the words,
and then I know

just how my father
felt when he was working
late in the garage

at his tool bench
carving old-fashioned
wooden toys

for my first born,
squinting hard to place
the pegs and pieces

in just the right spots
so the car's wheels
would spin or the dog's

legs would wobble,
making my son laugh.

First Basket

You are nine years old,
I am standing, winter coat
still on, leaning against
the wall of the gymnasium
at Henry James School
on the first day of Y ball,
the first game of your life.

The mechanical clock
begins to tick, the other
team shoots and misses,
you dribble the ball up
the floor cut to your right
cross over to your left
drive down the center
of the lane score a basket.

I turn to your mother,
my smile wide as the hoop
itself, say "That's my boy"
not realizing then that
the years would fly by and
the games would all end
before that ball could even
hit the floor to bounce
up into my waiting hands.

Grandma's Words

Every evening after the dinner dishes
had been washed and dried, and the kitchen table wiped,
my grandmother would sit alone and play Boggle,
shaking the dice like a professional gambler,
her eyes closed tight—a prayer perched silently on her lips—
and after the letters came tumbling out,
a scattering of possibilities,
for a moment the room would be absolutely still.

She had lived in a silent world for decades,
shouting and pointing her way through a widow's life,
opinionated and stubborn, as tough as the rails
her husband had ridden for thirty years,
let everyone know what she thought of Pete Rose—that little shit—
fiercely loyal to her town, her Pirates, her family.

But when she played with words at that kitchen table,
she became a different person—an artist—a collector of odd words.
Mizzle. Diluvium. Collet. Ternary. Sussurate.
Sometimes I would watch her stare at the spilled letters
like an oracle, as if she could move them around with her eyes,
rearrange them, imagine for them new permutations,
create sounds out of the silence of her life,
meanings out of those wooden cubes strewn across the shine.

Learning to Dance

Our neighbor's older sister
        taught us all how to slow dance
                when we were in the 6th grade.

After school, we'd cross the road,
        run straight into their tiny house
                (only five minutes from St. Aloysius)

and gather there in the darkened
        basement, four 12-year-old boys
                and a tall, pretty 14-year-old girl

who already knew how to sway
        her body seductively to the 45's
                undulating on her record player,

who would take us one by one
        by our hands into the still center
                of the room and spin us slowly

around and around, like records
        on a turntable, until we could hear
                only the music and our breathing.

She was old enough to wear lipstick
        and perfume, but I was too young,
                too scared, to wrap myself around her.

Proof Positive

At my age
(don't even ask me)
we all talk
about how much time
has sped up
(the older we all get,
the faster it flies)

and it's only a joke,
of course,
that ocean of night
just ahead
having now focused
our thoughts
like a mortal lens,

but today I discover
it's true
and here's the proof:
I'm out riding
along the Cape Cod
Rail Trail
(trying to keep

my old heart racing)
when I glance
to the left
at a surprising sound,
a squirrel skirring
or a bobolink
flashing through the pines,

and in an instant
I find myself swerving
off the path headlong into bayberry,
toppling over
a hidden embankment
into dune grass.

Why, when
I was a teenager
(only a few
thousand heartbeats ago)
I could stare
for hours and hours
at sinuous girls

in their tight shorts
strutting down
the shiny sidewalks while
I glided past
in my ordinary car
without ever even thinking
I might crash.

The Age of Transistors

My father gave me a transistor radio kit
for my birthday when I turned seven

(transistor radios still cost a bundle then
but you could get a kit for half price),

and I watched as he stared at the schematic
under the glare of the electric lantern,

turning back and forth from the sheet
to the tiny board spread out there

on his workbench, holding the gun
in his right hand, the solder in his left,

an acrid smell looping through the garage
as I looked on mesmerized and afraid.

In my bedroom later that day I pressed
my ear to the radio to hear the tinny sounds

barely audible even after I had switched
the volume all the way up to high,

so I took an old piece of scrap wire,
twisted one end into a hole in the radio

and then pushed the frazzled other end
straight into the socket on the wall.

Vectors of fire spliced through my fingers
as the radio flew through the air:

my first introduction to the vast powers
of the brave new digital world.

Escape

The doors of St. Aloysuis
opened like magic
and boys and girls rushed
into the sunlight

of an unusually warm
October afternoon
screaming and shouting
and leaping up

to celebrate Mazeroski's
walk-off home run.
Even the nuns had let
their classes listen

to the game on tiny
transistor radios
(except for maybe Sister
Wilbert's 6th grade)

and now there was no
escaping the fact
that sport could indeed
translate decades

of despair into wings,
the dark skies of Pittsburgh
bluer now than they had
ever been before

as all the city's children
skipped home.

That's Christmas to Me

It's only ten days before Christmas
and I'm sitting early at my desk listening
to the Pentatonix Christmas album
for the first time when all of a sudden
I laugh out loud as the five singers
do a mash-up of "Winter Wonderland"
and "Don't Worry, Be Happy."
This on a dark morning when the paper's
headlines speak of new gun violence,
this time at a Chocolate Cafe in Sydney
and I'm thinking December just can't
get any darker, but of course it can.
Tomorrow will bring the horrible news
of the school shooting in Pakistan. So
I know that we must look for wonder
wherever we can find it.
                          The last time
I saw my father was at Christmas
almost thirty years ago. I remember him,
propped up on his elbows on the living
room carpet, his heavy glasses hovering
at the tip of his nose, painstakingly building
an Ewok village with our seven-year-old
while I played Christmas songs on the organ,
joining the pieces as our son watched,
propped up on his elbows just like Grandpa,
the two of them creating a world purely
out of dreams of furry Wookies and cosmic
peace. That world, that room, was a place
where magic lived. Only six weeks later
my father was gone.
                          But if Christmas
means anything to me now, it's shining

in that memory that whispers to me across the years. Sometimes we can take the worries of our world and transform them into wonderlands just like the Forest Moon of Endor—a Sanctuary Moon— where for a day or a moment or even a season, we can forget about the Death Star and dance together in the trees.

Christmas Lights

Every year on a Saturday morning in December
my mother would bundle us in our puffy coats
and my father would pack us into the family car

so the "boys" could do their Christmas shopping.
We'd peer out the windows at smiling Santas
teetering on the roofs of stores and homes along

East Ohio Street, or strings of lights criss-crossing
the avenues of Lawrenceville. We were looking
for shiny pots and pans for our mother, and maybe

a scarf, too, though our father always made
a quick stop at one of the jewelry marts scattered
amongst the shops. I remember sliding through

ice tunnels holding hands with my brothers and
I remember how the stores all smelled like Christmas,
but most of all I remember the lights dazzling

in the air above the grimy streets of Pittsburgh
back when all it took was a wave of magic
to remake the world. Today people everywhere

pay money to drive their cars through Holiday
Fantasias, high-tech extravaganzas with millions
of flashing bulbs, but I hold fast to memories

of being tucked tight in the back seat of that old
Plymouth with my three brothers as our father
guided us along city streets where angels and bells

and wreaths floated above us as the world turned
red and green and gold in the Christmas lights.

My Friend's Granddaughter Discovers Rain

She's standing there
      at the edge of the awning,
            her feet on the dry patio,

her right hand stretched
      out into the falling rain
            cautiously opening and

closing her fingers
      trying to catch the drops
            then looking down to see

the splashing sounds
      she hears there, then out
            again at her hand cupping

the tiny raindrops
      backing up just a little
            before stepping straight

into the rain, letting
      it drip down her cheeks,
            her face alive in wonder,

turning her hands up
      and down, glancing
            at him with a sudden smile.

Changing Names

My daughter went away to college and changed her name.
When we called to leave her a message on her birthday,
she was in Vancouver at a jam band concert.
Because there was no voice mail box for Emily, we almost hung up.
"This is Autumn," the voice chirped instead,
"I'm not in, so leave a message and I'll get back to you." Right.
Autumn, the middle name she'd always despised.

Everyone who knows us thinks we named our daughter
for Emily Dickinson, a poet for whom words were tiny treasures,
amethysts and dewdrops, little vials holding the essence of amazing sense,
but the truth is we just liked the sound of a simple old-fashioned name.
In fact, we decided early on to call her *Emily Elizabeth,*
but sunlight sprayed the air so brightly that October day she was born
that no one could believe winter would ever come:
so she was, it seems, a child of autumn's sweetest breezes,
and Autumn she would become.

I'm pleased my daughter has found her own name.
I hope she lets this name guide her through the seasons,
a name that embodies change itself, a time of piercing electricity
when everything and everyone lives on high alert,
the birds winging like lasers through the air,
in the final surge of life before all the great world turns to bone.

Cherish your new name, child, hold it always in your heart,
let it be your moon and your sun and your stars.
If it is true that you must change your life, as Rilke once wrote,
then the very first step must be—can only be—
to change your name.

Song for January 2

There was a DJ and dancing
in the Red Barn two nights ago
at Holcomb Farm, a party
to celebrate the confluence
of birthdays and anniversaries
and the arrival of the new year,
long-held kisses and noisemakers
at the stroke of midnight too,
but tonight as I drive home
across the snow-swept campus
I see the Wolf Moon rising
above the darkened mounds
of Barndoor Hills, a golden
circle so large I think I could
step onto it and see the whole
world spread out before me
as the days begin their simple
journey from dark to light
to dark and back to light again.

II. LESSONS OF THE GAME

The Infidels Come to Church

The Infidels invaded Trinity Episcopal Church
        just as the memorial service was beginning,

walking quickly, but silently, along the nave
        and slipping into the first row of the transept

where they stared politely ahead as the oboeist
        began to play Bach's haunting "Sheep May Safely

Graze," all five of them balding and bearded
        and brawny with their club's name, *Infidels,*

stenciled on the backs of their leather jackets,
        and although I could easily imagine the mayhem

the five could produce—heads cracked open,
        glass strewn on the road—really, if they had only

exchanged their jackets for cassocks, I could also
        have seen them as monks gathered for morning

prayers in an abbey, and not as the riding
        buddies of the deceased woman's eldest son—

also balding and bearded and brawny—
        and in fact it brought me some quiet peace

to watch the Infidels staring meditatively
        at the sanctuary as members of the woman's

family read from the Bible and others
        played other consoling pieces of music.

Later at the reception I came to the buffet
        table just as one of the Infidels arrived

there too, both of us reaching forward
        to grab one of the delicious mini-Reubens,

so I thanked him for coming to the service,
        noticing his soft eyes, and he spoke in a kind

voice of being sorry to arrive so late,
        but the downpour on the Mass Pike

had made it difficult to steer his Harley,
        and then he padded back to the bench

where the five Infidels quietly ate finger
        sandwiches and sipped glasses of punch.

I myself am no longer a man of faith,
        but it was difficult for me not to bow

in awe to the mysteries of death and life
        that had brought us here—infidels and

believers alike—on this rainy Halloween
        morning to this church in the conformity

of grief that finally and everlastingly
        makes brothers and sisters of us all.

Lessons of the Game

1. Never Throw the Third Strike
Down the Center of the Plate

I was pitching for the Phillies
on a Saturday morning in May
with the bright sun as an ally
glinting hard over my shoulder.

It was the top of the seventh
and I had a no-hitter going.
(Who would've guessed that
the skinny ten-year-old boy

on the mound was as close then
to perfection as he would ever be?)
With two outs, the next batter,
the biggest boy in the whole

fourth grade, stared at me from
the box, but I was on fire that day,
whipping the ball like the wind,
and just like that the count was

0-2, and so I turned my back
once more to gather my strength.
One more pitch, one more pitch . . .
I was so captivated by the cheers

of anticipated glory that I didn't
hear my coach, my Uncle Bill,
trying frantically to catch my
attention, so I just rocked back

and let loose another fastball,
right down the middle,
and I couldn't even spin around
fast enough to see that ball land.

My Uncle walked to the mound,
told me to take a deep breath,
suggested using a change-up
every once in awhile, and then

left me there to finish the game.
I can't even remember who won.
Deception, surprise, strategy,
keeping the hitters guessing—

these are the lessons we learn,
eventually, the compensations
for speed and power and youth,
for all those games that follow

one after another as we move
from field to field to field.

2. Throwing Strikes Is Harder Than It Looks

My father was the manager of my team,
the Braves of the Reserve Township Little League,
and I got to play all the choicest positions:

short stop, catcher and, of course, pitcher too.
On the very last day of the season, we were playing
the Yankees for the right to go to the playoffs.

The score was tied as we began the bottom
of the seventh at 8-8. I had had a couple of hits,
and a few nice plays in the field. I felt good

about our chances. Two outs and three
base runners later, my Dad sauntered slowly
to the mound and called on me to come in

to face the next batter, to get the last out.
I felt great in warm-ups, not nervous at all,
the ball popping into the catcher's mitt,

picked by my own father to win the game.
My first pitch was a high fastball; then a ball
inside and low made the count 2-0.

(I took a deep breath and looked around
the diamond. All I could hear were the shouts
of parents and kids, a city park filled

with the noise of the game.) My third
pitch was high again and I felt everything
slow down. My Dad cried out to me

"Relax, step back, just throw strikes,"
but I knew it was all over, I'd blown the game,
our playoff chances, my Dad's faith

in me—I couldn't have thrown a strike
in a million years—and as I watched that
Yankee cross the plate, my tears fell.

I saw a chasm open up between dream
and reality. In that moment I knew exactly
what my growing up would be all about.

3. Don't Get Comfortable, It's Such a Long Season

We moved to a new house in the suburbs
the summer after my sophomore year in high school.

The baseball season had already begun, of course,
but my Dad managed to finagle a try-out for me

with the Ross Township Pony League team.
So on a sunny Saturday morning in June I arrived

at one of the local elementary schools and found
my way to the baseball field. After talking a little while

with the coach about my credentials, I started
warming up with a few of the guys on the team.

Then the coach set up a scrimmage and kept me
in at the cage to take a couple of swings at the plate.

I was the third batter up. The first two had made outs,
a pop up to first and a weak grounder to second.

I stepped casually into the batter's box, adjusted
my helmet, took a few quick practice swings, and

stared out at the pitcher. The first pitch was a fastball
right across the center of the plate, and I attacked it,

lining the ball into left center field. I rounded
first base smartly, with my eye on the cut-off man,

but decided to settle for a sharp single. The pitcher
went to the stretch to hold me on the base, but I danced

a little off the bag to discompose him a bit.
He threw a ball into the dirt, but the catcher blocked it.

When he stood to return the ball to the pitcher,
I broke on his throw and dashed quickly to second base,

arriving safely before the pitcher even knew
what was happening. The coach nodded in approval,

and I knew I had won a place on the team.
The rest of that practice went well, and I picked up

my uniform before heading home with Dad.
On Tuesday evening, I was starting for the team

in center field and batting third in the order. I lined
a base hit to right field in my first official at bat.

It was the last hit I would have for over a month.
Instead, I got myself picked off first base by a leftie,

set a local record for consecutive pop ups, and
misjudged a fly ball to center so badly that it bounced

about forty feet off my forehead. A lot of things
can go wrong in baseball. It's such a long, long season.

Watching My Son Bathe His Son

Bedtime for my first grandson
and I'm watching his father, my son,

bathe him at the kitchen counter,
testing the water to get the temperature

just right, placing the baby shampoo
and the miniature washcloth right

beside the newborn's bath tub, gently
lowering his son into the water,

all the while whispering soft words
to his baby boy, and suddenly

I am back in that tiny apartment
on Hope Street with him, my son,

lowering him so tentatively
into the water, afraid of letting

him slip and fall, afraid of hurting
what I didn't even know how

to love yet, wondering if I knew
how to bathe an infant, wondering

if I could ever be the kind of father
who might teach his son just

what it means to care for a child.

Altars

I worship at the altar of the line
break, the poet says in an interview
and I get it—stopping, starting,
turning are the boundary markers
of the changes that shape our lives.
Of course, she could have said the altar
of the image, too, crisp and new,
fraught with implications and the sharp
sensual moments that bring us to
our knees or to new understandings.
Or what about the altar of the metaphor
ripping new meanings from old cloth,
grabbing you by the throat and spinning
you around in a dizzying dance of words?
Then there are all those other altars:
the chiseled stones of ancient cathedrals
or the woven mats of a hermit's hut,
and, of course, many a man or woman
has worshipped at the altar of the beloved's
lips or the needle's crazy addictive song
or the no-one's-ever-been-here-before vista
of a staggering wilderness. In fact,
there are altars everywhere in time and
space, in memory and in desire; the key is
simply to look for them and worship.

Consciousness Bars

We're off to see an indie movie
        on a lovely summer evening, so she
                dashes into the market to get us

a few not-so-healthy-for-us treats
        while I sit in the car daydreaming,
                the one life skill I've really mastered,

until suddenly a huge black Lexus
        pulls silently into the slot next to ours
                and I glance at its door: *Starwinds,*

says the writing, *unlock your possibilities.*
        Which is just what I've always wanted,
                a chance to unleash my inner possibilities.

But how can I do this, that's the question?
        Well, I need look no further than the Lexus's
                door which advertises Reiki Sound Therapy

and Tuning Fork Therapy as ways
        to access consciousness bars, sure
                to work for novices and experts alike,

to open pathways to deep harmony
        with the universe. In fact, later I discover
                that the internet is full of helpful suggestions,

not to mention numerous web sites
        offering to tune me up for a (modest) charge.
                Why there's even the Atlantis College of Crystal

and Sound Healing if I really want
        to immerse myself in therapeutic sounds.
                So there it is: after all these years, the truth

emerges: I've simply never had access
        to enough consciousness bars, and so,
                tone-deaf and clueless, I've drifted tunelessly

through all my nights and days
        in a wilderness without consciousness,
                without access to the music of the stars.

Living in a Poem

If it is true that each of us
is living in a poem
then I must be at the exact
center of the beginning
of that poem today, down
low on my hands and knees
in a community garden
completely overrun by three
weeks of weeds growing
wild, with a little digger
in one hand, an orange plastic
basket by my side, drawing
the dirt into my bones, trying
to finger the tiny green seedlings
of squashes and peppers all
but strangled by waves of iron
chickweed, the sun an enormous
yellow ball of fire somewhere
in the distant dome of the sky,
bluer now than the deepest
waters, the wind when it comes
an unspoken promise, just me
and the work left to be done here
in the center of the garden.

Bagging a Deer

It's the only way I'd ever get one, really.
I mean, sure I dimly remember firing an M16,

lying on my stomach at the ROTC rifle range
in college, right before I became a Peacenik.

Other than that, though, I've never even touched
a firearm of any kind. But my father-in-law,

a Korean War veteran, was a hunter,
and I had stared at that buck's head on the wall

in the family room for decades,
those liquid eyes watching as we'd play

ping pong to while away the evening's hours.
Now, over a year after his death,

my wife's sister is trying to clean out
the house, getting rid of everything she can.

So she's unmounted the head and wrapped it
in a black plastic trash bag,

which I am now stuffing into my car's trunk
to take back home to Connecticut

where in a few weeks I'll mount it
on pegboard in the basement,

the first and only time I will have ever
bagged a deer.

Whenever I asked him about his time
in the war, my father-in-law

would sit back and say, "Son, you really don't
want to hear about what happened

over there." Then he'd close his eyes and sigh.
That sigh is what I'll hear whenever I go

down to the basement and glimpse that buck
guarding all the quiet darkness.

Only a Rat's Life

Scientists at some modern university,
with its high-tech labs and rooms full of computers,
have just announced, after years of experiments,
that rats who are forced to subsist on near-starvation diets
and who make do completely without exercise and sex,
live to extraordinary ages, some achieving almost
twice the life-expectancy of your average rat.

So I guess I'm supposed to extrapolate:
without food and sex I too could gain astounding
longevity. And isn't that just what I've always
wanted, to live on the very edge of hunger,
to become so dull that I forget the colors of desire,
the fierce need to taste and swallow,
how it feels to have to gasp for my next breath
as I lie beside my lover in the dawn
of a cloudless Sunday morning?

I can imagine a worse fate, though.
I could have been one of those unlucky rats,
plopped down in a tiny cage in the lab
without even a thimble for an exercise wheel,
fed indiscriminate servings of unseasoned pellets,
not even allowed to riffle through a rat's *Playboy*
during my long and empty days,
my slow and senseless nights.

Birds of New Zealand

The Kaka stares at me through gnarled
branches only about an arm's length away,
deciding whether to speak or remain
silent when all of a sudden he cries "Kaa,
Kaa-Ka" and stares insistently at me,
maybe expecting an alien's curious reply.
But before I can even imagine a word
I might say to him, he breaks into a string
of whistles and moans and clicks
punctuated at the end by a loud "Kraak"!
He is speaking a language I simply
don't understand, so eventually I turn
to continue walking down the path,
wondering if such a misunderstanding
marked the encounters of giant Moas
with New Zealand's first humans
only eight or nine hundred years ago.
Without any fear, or any defenses,
those giant Moas were extinct within
a couple of centuries while today the Kaka,
beautiful parrots who ruled the forests
of all three islands for millennia, have
dwindled to only 10,000, though the hope
is they will survive in protected reserves
like Zealandia where I am hiking now
with my daughter. So many birds—so many
species—gone because we could not
learn to speak their languages.

Foolish Assumptions Again

The two of us are sitting in a booth
at Ken's Corner Breakfast and Lunch
after a morning of picking blueberries
at our favorite pick-your-own farm
when I glance over to see a young
man, no more than a burly boy really,
standing in the aisle with his back
facing me, his left arm riddled
with dark swirls of tattoos, wearing
a backwards baseball cap, just
another irreverent punk taking up
space in an otherwise wholesome
café in Glastonbury, that's what I'm
thinking to myself,
                        but then he shifts
his feet lightly and swings to his left
and I see that he has a one-month-old
baby cradled in that arm. The child's
mother is sitting across from me
staring up at the boy with enough love
to save the whole damn world, but
for now the boy himself has eyes only
for his tiny child who is fixed on
his father's face, not the dark tattoos,
not the crooked baseball cap, just
his father's eyes. And then I hear
the waitress whisper to the pretty girl,
"Bet you never thought you'd see that!"

Sunflowers

Not far from where there's a massive manhunt
for the survivalist who ambushed two state policemen
a few weeks ago, my wife and I were driving back
to Pittsburgh to visit her mother earlier in the summer.

We'd decided to forsake the usual high-speed
highways, I-80 or the PA Turnpike, and so we were
driving along two-lane country back roads on
a July day of shimmering sunshine and pristine air

when we rounded a bend, wildflower meadows
on our left, rolling hills on our right, and saw
a sign saying something about an Amish farmstead
up ahead. One more bend revealed that farm

with an old-fashioned fence bordered by a couple
of rows of resplendent sunflowers that, as we
got closer, revealed themselves to be not several rows
of sunflowers but an entire field of them and then,

just as we reached the stone and wood house,
built on a rise, we gasped to see fields and fields
of sunflowers spreading behind the house for
acres and acres all the way to the edge of the woods.

It was a stunning vision of beauty and harmony
that stayed in our minds like the sweetest
of dreams until three days later when we took
my mother-in-law to the Pittsburgh Zoo,

located in Highland Park, a mostly urban area
of the city. On the way home, I glanced at

some of those narrow triple-decker Pittsburgh
houses carved right into the hillsides,

rundown wooden homes that looked the same
now as they had when I was a kid living
in the North Hills of Pittsburgh over fifty years
ago, embodiments of the poverty and grit

people always associate with steel mill towns.
Those homes all have steep concrete steps
leading to the doors and little patches of lawn
in front of those steps, but this one house

that caught my attention did not have a yard:
instead there was a ten-by-ten little field
of towering sunflowers, a golden flag waving
in a concrete world, shouting, Y*es, here too,*

even here, there is beauty and harmony, and
I could see how that Amish farm and this
city tenement both spoke of our most human
need to find something beautiful to praise.

My Grandson Sends Me a Text Message

Even though he's only a little over three
his parents already refer to him as a screenager

(he's living in a very bookish family, too
but phones and iPads and laptops are absolutely

ubiquitous these days), and he is already
adept at watching truck videos or pushing the red

button to end FaceTime calls or just recently
sending lines of letters and numbers in coded text

messages like the ones he sent to me last
weekend when my wife was babysitting for him,

messages like *fyqooolzxx3m7jjka##)pxz,*
accompanied by strings of emoji's, what he calls

faces, lots of smiley ones of course, but now
that he's discovered other pictures, he asks her,

"Does Pappap like pizza? Does he like beer?"
And what follows is a string of foods and drinks

until at last he laughs to see one he calls
a "mountain of chocolate," and with delight

he adds that one to his next text.

Pickup Game on Elmgrove Street

August in Providence, way too hot to read Foucault.
So my friend Mark and I decide to shoot some hoops,
hop in his beat-up car, and head out Hope Street,
looking for a little friendly competition,
but no one's playing at Hope High today, and besides
the courts are in terrible shape, bent rims and potholes everywhere,
so we drive on down towards Wayland Square.

Not too far from the university's gymnasium
there's a little public park with a smooth asphalt court.
The hoops there are strung with metal nets
that glisten today in the summer's incessant sun.
Two black kids are shooting around,
jive-talking and laughing, when we walk in,
ask if they want to play a little game of two-on-two.
(Their rusted bicycles lie in a twisted heap next to the gate.)
They size us up: two skinny white guys wearing glasses,
too obviously intellectual to know any real moves,
to be able to handle the ball like candy or to shoot like silk.
Sure, show us what you got!

We strip off our already drenched shirts and begin.
The boys are quicker but the two of us have played more ball:
we know how to execute the pick and roll,
how to hit the cutter with a deftly placed bounce pass.
When that fails, I drain a few jumpers, or Mark drives to the hole.
"Who do you guys think you are, Havlicek and West?"
one of the boys asks, and we all laugh.
Mark and I win the first game, but they take the second.
Then we all decide, without saying a word,
to take a break and sit in the shade of the scrawny trees
by the barely working water fountain,

two grad students from Brown and two Hope High boys,
winded and happy, against a chain-link fence.

Soon, we're playing the third game for all the glory.
The ball feels so good now, so real and purposeful to me,
that for a while all thoughts of libraries and papers
dissolve in the shimmering air.
All I know is I'm on the court hanging out with the guys,
making the summer go by,
lifting the ball again and again in perfect arcs
toward the solar rims.

I'll never see these kids again,
or remember their names even if they told us them.
Tomorrow I'll crank up the old dilapidated air conditioner,
and get back to *Gravity's Rainbow*.
But today's game is not about winning or losing—
it's just about playing, the flow of bodies on a hot asphalt court,
the bumping and pushing, the hard cuts and jump stops,
the shooting and talking in the summer's heat.

"Nice shot," I finally say, to all of us
as the game ends and we all high-five each other.
"Catch you later," I hear one boy say quietly
though we all know we'll never see each other again.
Mark winks a smile at me and we slip off,
jump into his car to head home.

III. LAST LIGHT

Last Light

In the last light of this April evening
the branches of the trees outside my window

stitch themselves—black on black—
into the dark cloak of night.

Even fifteen minutes ago I could see
forsythia—yellow and green—

and the sun's diminuitive reflection
off the windows of my neighbor's house.

Before that, the sunlight splashed
against the ocean's water where I played

with my brothers, or burst like music
into the dappled woods behind our house.

All that light back then, all that shining,
spread over the yard as my father and uncles

pitched to us late into the summer's night
while my mother and aunts sat circled

in folding chairs talking, laughing so loud
we thought they'd wake the dead.

Now, as sudden as the first breath of fall,
night has arrived with its absences,

and I can barely make out anything at all
except the quiet beauty of the last light.

Seeing My Father Again

Yesterday I caught a glimpse of my father
dead for over a decade. He was walking down
the main street of the town I live in now.

I think he looked up just as I drove by,
with perhaps the merest hint of recognition,
then wavered away into the busy crowd.

This is not the first time I've seen him
since he died: sometimes he appears to me
as an older version of the man I knew,

grayer, thinner too, sometimes he's younger
and walks briskly away from me, sometimes I see
only a dim resemblance, as if he were only

a distant cousin newly arrived from Greece.
Always I want to stop him, ask him what it's like
to be dead, talk to him about my life now,

show him pictures of the grandchildren
he remembers only as tiny babies, and the one
he doesn't even know exists, tell him

I miss him, quiz him about the queer ways
of movement in that other world that allow him
to grow older and younger at the same time.

But always he disappears, turns a corner,
drives steadily away in the opposite direction,
and I fear that I will never see him again.

An Ordinary Evening in Hartford

4:30 PM on the shortest day of the year
and I am driving up Avon Mountain
in the darkening light of the fast fading day
with my daughter sitting beside me
lost in her own thoughts, when suddenly—
without thinking really—I look up to see
burgeoning circles of color, textured
in cobalt and mauve, everywhere the sky
arranging different worlds, feathered clouds
slipping through secret windows, a sky
so spectacular in satin grays and deepening blues,
so alive in its final seconds of existence
that I lose my breath for a moment—
I know this scene will never happen again,
has never happened anywhere before—
there will never be a sky so full of differences,
so full of possibilities, and I will never feel
this alive again.   Two hours later, I walk
in the chilled darkness of winter's first night
to my next door neighbor's Christmas party.
He greets me with a look of animal anxiety
and draws me aside to tell me he has bad news.
A friend of mine died just hours ago
after returning home from an afternoon jog—
the very afternoon of those fantastic colors—
and just like that I am drowned in the quotidian:
this too will never happen again, has never
happened before, is utterly irredeemable.
I move through the evening's celebrations

ashamed to hold my life, to have felt so alive
at that awful moment, to be eating and drinking
now, talking casually with friends, laughing.
My friend is dead, the winter has come on,
the sky will never spin in wheels again.

On Books and Death

When my father died, so unexpectedly,
I was reading Whitman's poetry.

Even today the sound of little waves
paddling against a ferryboat,

the gleam of sunlight whispering
off the water, or an older man's face

turned suddenly towards me can bring
him back so entirely I have to gasp

to catch my breath. Coming home
from my mother's funeral in Pittsburgh

I was reading the "Spring" chapter of Walden
and now the simple shattering of ice,

the first translucent threads of wildflowers,
or March's sudden shifting moods

carry my mother home again to me.
So just in case death drops by here today,

with all his insouciance and usual bad timing,
remember me in the books you love.

First Snow

It's mid-November
        and the last leaves hang
                half on half off the trees;

everything seems suspended
        today, the sky a gunmetal grey
                pockmarked by thin splotches

of pale blue, and you call
        "Come, look at the sky," so
                I slip on my shoes and turn

the corner into the yard only
        to stare at nothing I can see
                because what is invisible

is invisible until it's not,
        like the first line of dawn
                before there is any glimmer

of light or the blush
        of love before you've even
                imagined your lips brushing,

so it takes me a while
        to see the miniscule dots
                of pure white like so many

shooting stars flashing
        against the grey-blue
                canvas of November's sky.

Bent Rims and Flat Tires

When the snow falls
      as soft as baby's breath
in the quiet stillness
      of December's whisperings,
no one is thinking
      about the sheets of ice
weighing down roads
      like ponderous glaciers
all through January and
      February and even March,
because it's all so pretty
      at first, all so romantic—
cups of mulled cider,
      sitting in the fire's glow—
no one is seeing then
      the shattered macadam,
the deep ruts and craters
      ready to swallow cars up
whole when the earth
      turns warm once again,
all those bent rims
      and flat tires already
there in the first flakes.

Sooner or Later

Imagining where to edge
a new flower bed
I discover the buried bricks
that marked yours
already nearly two inches under
the encroaching grass.

April is a cruel month indeed:
everywhere the shoots
are pushing up, everywhere
the blossoms burst into sunlight,
the Japanese cherry
paints the air with pink perfumes,

but all this life—sooner
or later—will turn back to rock,
two inches deep and already
I feel the pressure of miles of stone,
look up to see the branches
turning to bone.

Going Under

Today I went into Hartford
for what's called in the med business
a little "procedure," the fourth
of its kind I've had since turning fifty,

and you might think the nasty
part was the day and a half of prep,
but in fact that all goes smoothly
now, though it's not something any

one wants to talk about and I
wouldn't say it's a pleasure. No,
the truly scary part is the going
under, and not because the drugs

are painful or the experience
itself scarily unsettling. In fact,
I was surrounded by pretty
women talking softly and doing

whatever they could to make me
comfortable, and I was only
out for what seemed like a minute,
even though the clock said it

was more like an hour. No, what gave
me a start again was the thought
that being out also felt like an eternity,
and I knew I might never

have come back to this life, the sweet
sounds of the recovery room like

the voices of angels as I sipped my
ginger ale and munched on a cracker,

happy to be awake now in this world
and knowing someday I won't.

Skin on Skin

He arrives just before noon
to take her to the cafeteria for lunch,
just as he does every Tuesday,
and has done for more than a year now,

and walks down the hall to her room,
sits softly in the chair as she stares
at him for over a minute before saying,
"Do I know you?"—his wife

of almost fifty years—nevertheless
he smiles at her, identifies himself again,
takes her by the arm, and leads her
to the center's cafeteria. As they enter

he sees the silver-headed man, once
a bishop he's been told, motion
to his wife to join him. He was leading
her there anyway, so he guides her

to the seat next to the man, who puts
his hand firmly on top of hers and
does not remove it. She smiles at him
affectionately, basking in the only

comfort left for her now, the solace
of skin on skin.

The Cells of Your Heart

Of the trillions and trillions of cells
that make up your body

the only ones that have been with you
since the day you were born

and that will still be with you
on the day that you die

can be found in your flashing lens
and in the deepest layers

of your brain, which all makes
perfect evolutionary sense of course,

though based on what I know
and what I've seen

I would've guessed those immutable
cells would be buried

in the twisting pathways of your heart
where your darkest secrets

and deepest desires are trapped forever
and where all your tears have no

beginning and no end.

The Milky Way

I am standing
      in the middle of
           Observatory Field

on the darkest night
      of summer, staring
           straight up at the sky

trying to see
      the Milky Way,
           something I've tried

to do all my life
      without success
           (to be perfectly honest

I've always had
      trouble finding Orion
           or even the Big Dipper)

so the only images
      of the Milky Way
           I know of are those

luminous photos
      you see in books
           about astronomy.

What I see instead
      are innumerable stars
           swimming in an ocean

of black, a totally
          random wash of light
                    spread in every direction,

and I know our galaxy
          is only one of billions
                    of galaxies flying away

from us at ineffable
          velocities, but still
                    detectable, and still

beautiful beyond words
          even if I myself can't
                    see the Milky Way.

What is shocking
          is to know that
                    were I to swish

ahead a few billion
          years, I'd be able
                    only to see the stars

in the Milky Way,
          all the others having
                    disappeared from view.

The Milky Way will
          be the only universe
                    our distant descendants

will know at all
          unless somehow records
                    from our time survive —

    such a diminished
           universe yet filled
                  with all the beauty

of the galaxy
        I cannot even see
                in my own universe.

The Garden in September

After summer's endless rains I don't really
expect anything but riot and decay
when I go down to the community garden
to see if there's anything left to pick

but instead I'm surprised to see so much
profusion and new growth: yard long green beans
still hanging from poles, arugula sprouting
beside the mounds of thyme and Greek oregano,

zinnias and glads still blooming, still awash
with new buds, tomatoes everywhere on vines
that hung empty throughout the summer,
a thousand hot peppers hanging upside down

on spreading bushes the size of small trees.
What force is it that pushes these plants
to grasp for autumn's now diminished light
even in the midst of so much collapse?

The garden has always been a classroom
for me, but the lessons I learn there
are never the ones I think I'll be learning.
Life in the garden is one surprise after another.

Night Light

Nothing is really any different this morning:
the book of poems and the glass of water
still sit on my bedside table just where I left them
before switching off the light after you'd fallen asleep;
your scarves, splashes of indigo, taupe and crimson,
still hang fluted from wooden pegs on the wall;
and I still can hear the dull thrumming of the fan
hidden in the attic window above our bedroom.
Outside, the shadows of the pines dart in the air,
the chimes, like shiny bangles, clang in the breezeway,
the birds sing for their breakfasts by the feeder.
Our three children lie sleeping in their own rooms
(naturally, it is only the middle of the night for them).
Nothing at all has really changed this morning.

Still, last night in the very instant before sleep,
I felt your touch in the hollow of my back,
stirring me awake, spinning me into your arms,
just the way it used to happen, often, always—
I felt your body opening to me, sparking the darkness,
making it all just disappear, disappear forever.
Only moments ago the sun uncloaked the earth,
not with the light of some divine transformation,
blasting the forests and rifting the mountains,
but with ordinary light, the light we rarely stop to see,
light that begins in dawn and effortlessly guides us
through our days, spending its magic little by little
even in the blackest hours of midnight bedrooms,
so that somehow for us each day is new.

Sleep Machine

Lying under the covers
still halfway between dream
and awake, I'm listening
to the ocean sounds of the sleep
machine while my fingers
glide softly along your thigh,
remembering those nights
we spent on the Outer Banks,
exploring shores we'd only
imagined, the water's crashing
echoing our cries, our joy.

Surprise

Yesterday
walking home
heavy with the day's
thousand little failures,
I saw a brilliant ball emerge
from the thick pines at the edge
of the fields, its red and blue
stripes rising breathlessly
up into the docile sky,
just as you appeared
that first moment
you floated
into my
life.

ABOUT THE AUTHOR

A life-long reader and long-time high school English teacher, Michael Cervas has always been at home in the world of books and ideas. Although he only began writing poems in his forties, he has discovered that the surest way to seek the dawn is to open every door. Accordingly, he tries hard to open those doors to produce his own work and to inspire his students, too, so that they can see the world through the eyes of poets and the lens of poetry. In addition to teaching language and literature, Michael curates the Westminster Poetry Series (which began in 1999) and the Fridays at Westminster Series of Readings (which began in 2008), both of which bring contemporary writers and their works into the lives of his students. As correlative pleasures to reading and writing poetry, Michael enjoys music (he plays keyboards in an eclectic band), sports (he plays squash as often as possible), and nature (he oversees the community garden at Westminster). He and his wife Deborah live in the West End of Hartford, where they continue to work part-time as educators and full time as grandparents.

This book is set in Garamond Premier Pro, which had its genesis in 1988 when type-designer Robert Slimbach visited the Plantin-Moretus Museum in Antwerp, Belgium, to study its collection of Claude Garamond's metal punches and typefaces. During the mid-fifteen hundreds, Garamond—a Parisian punch-cutter—produced a refined array of book types that combined an unprecedented degree of balance and elegance, for centuries standing as the pinnacle of beauty and practicality in type-founding. Slimbach has created an entirely new interpretation based on Garamond's designs and on compatible italics cut by Robert Granjon, Garamond's contemporary.

For more concerning the work of Michael Cervas, visit
www.antrimhousebooks.com/authors.html
This book is available at all bookstores
including Amazon.

www.ingramcontent.com/pod-product-compliance
Lightning Source LLC
Chambersburg PA
CBHW030159100526
44592CB00009B/357